The Chain Breaking Grave Bandit

A SERMON BY
Joey Grizzle

The Chain Breaking Grave Bandit

Published by Joey Grizzle

© 2020 Joey Grizzle

Cover design by: ZaoMedia, LLC

Photo by Jaanus Jagomägi on Unsplash

Printed in the United States of America

For permission contact: jgrizzle@bcog.me

Mark 5:1-6, "Then they came to the other side of the sea, to the country of the Gadarenes. And when He had come out of the boat, immediately there met Him out of the tombs a man with an unclean spirit, who had his dwelling among the tombs; and no one could bind him, not even with chains, because he had often been bound with shackles and chains. And the chains had been pulled apart by him, and the shackles broken in pieces; neither could anyone tame him. And always, night and day, he was in the mountains and in the tombs, crying out and cutting himself with stones. When he saw Jesus from afar, he ran and worshiped Him. And he cried out with a loud voice and said, "What have I to do with You, Jesus, Son of the Most High God?"

I am so delighted to have this passage in my heart. So much is going on in this Scripture that I think each one of you could use to make a profound difference in the way you approach God and in the way you approach life. There's something I like about this guy, and I've always tried to figure it out. I believe today, I have a little clarity. When I read about this fella in the tombs, I like the fact that everyone tried to put chains on him, and he kept breaking them. I like that everyone tried to lock him down, bound him up, and yet, he couldn't be locked; he couldn't be bound. He might not be saved, but at least, he's not controlled.

See, if I'm going to fight, let me fight the devil, but I'm not going to be owned by you. I may not have victory over my demons, but I will have victory over you. I may be wrestling against principalities and powers, but I'm not going to bow my knee to the chains of religion and the strong arm of flesh in my life.

No one could tame this man; no one could hold him back. This is what I'm praying for in my church, and this is what I'm praying for every person who reads this. I'm asking God to send us some untamed worshippers.

After all, I think that's why you may have picked up this sermon anyway. Pentecostals have a tendency to be drawn toward those things that are a little on the edge, and for those who aren't used to it, it can be an intriguing thing. We don't like our religion tame; we don't like our altar calls predictable, and we don't like our songs palatable. We like to have a moment in the presence of the Lord where you never know what God is going to do.

Matter of fact, many of you reading this may have picked this up just to break some rules. Something is stirring inside of you, and you've already made up your mind; something is about to change. It has to. How many of you weren't raised this way?

There's no reason for you, the way you were raised, to be coming into a Pentecostal church or reading a Pentecostal message like this, throwing your hands up, breaking chains, binding devils; you don't have any business doing all of that. Yet, you can feel it already. There's a thirst within your soul that has to be quenched, a longing for something more than you've had before. Well, today is your day.

Now honestly, I was raised this way. I've earned my pedigree to come and act crazy. I was raised around this stuff. But some of you, you were raised in a church that was as dead as four o'clock chicken on a Sunday afternoon. You don't have any business sitting in a Pentecostal House of Worship, but thanks be unto God, there's something about you that momma's little chain, that little, religious chain that was on you can't hold any longer. You're not worried about what they say anymore because you don't need a religion that is like what you had back then.

What you had back then led you to hell and back. What you want is something that will get you out of a graveyard, not one that will put you in the graveyard. See, there's some religion that belongs in the graves, but no, I need a chain-breaking religion! I'm asking God for a spirit of untamed praise to overwhelm us. I believe there will be a revival in our churches, as God begins sending sinners into the house who know that they're sinners.

This is the picture I have in my mind when I read this story: I see a Harley Davidson. I see a guy who has chains hanging off his belt buckle. I see a guy who has a leather vest that doesn't fit those muscles anymore. He can't fit in anything; chains can't hold him. His hair is too long; he's too rough, and he was raised wrong. I see a guy out there in a graveyard whom everyone has already rejected.

You might say, "Aw, people like that, they're just mean." No, they're out there crying; they're crying at night. The Bible says he was crying and cutting himself, sitting there punishing himself. He knows that he should be better. He knows that he should get fixed. He knows he should get off those drugs. He knows he should put his family back together. He knows he should be able to resist those temptations. He knows he ought to get his life right. Yet, he can't fix it; so, he just wounds it. He's out there in the graveyard hurting himself and cutting himself.

Don't you dare look down on people. Stop putting your chains on them. Do you know what your chains are? I'm talking about that stuff from which you're not free. I'm talking about those things that you hide from the public eye.

You've just grown comfortable in your own prison; so, you change your theology to accommodate your own backslidden condition, and you create converts who are twice the son of hell you are. You try and lock them down but let me tell you something. You can't run to Jesus if you're bound by the chains of religion.

Don't you look at people and say, "Aw, they can't be helped. They're too far gone. It's over. Just leave them in the graveyard. Don't go near them. They're crazy."

There is a witness writing this today who can say, "Thanks be unto God! He saved me!" God saved this wild man. God saved this woman (my wife) who was of a broken promise. The Lord brought me out of that graveyard, and the Lord brought her out of the darkness and set her free. We can testify!

Jesus is the one who gave me the strength to keep breaking chains until He showed up. I'm tired of the church putting chains on people. Now, don't equate rules with chains, either. Some of you are saying, "Yeah, I don't want any chains put on my life. That's why I have such a problem with church people." Well, dressing appropriately is not a chain. Telling you not to go to the bar is not a chain.

It's amazing what you can come up with to claim as a chain. You think any inhibition on your appetite is somehow a transgression on "true Christianity" in your lifestyle. The second the Lord speaks true Christianity into your life, you start rebuking it as if it's a demon. You proclaim, "You get that away from me. I'm not going to accept the burden of tithing. Tell me, I have to obey some rules, follow that pastor, and attend a church. No, I like to float around from church to church. I like to do what I want when I want and how I want!" That's a graveyard. Be careful; you may be trading chains for a grave.

Listen to me. A relationship has rules; religion has chains. "Pastor, a true relationship doesn't have rules." Okay, explain that to your wife. Go home and try that one out. Just call me when it gets over with. If I don't answer, just leave me a message, and I'll call you back. Yeah, if you accept the relationship, some rules go along with it. Only religion has chains.

I'll tell you what happened to too many guys in college. When I was there, I noticed a lot were raised in families steeped in ministry, and when they got to college, they really weren't… well, I didn't even know if they were Christians.

They didn't act like they loved God. They just kind of hung around God's stuff; then, when they graduated college, they needed a career. So, they chose the path they'd watched their father walk, but they didn't embrace it because of a calling and a passion for God. They simply embraced an opportunity.

I've seen these guys today. Some of them have authentic ministries now, and some of them have repented. Yet, a few of them, I still worry about because it seems to me, they rewrote the theology of the church to justify how they had acted in college. They rewrote their theology of God to compensate for how they want to live now. So, they get on stage and propagate a self-promoting gospel, and they wrap up all these people in the chains of their false doctrine. Then, when people leave the house, they leave with opinions rather than the Word of God. They leave with a doctrine that placates more to the comfort desires of their lifestyles than to the cross of Christ.

Many of you are loaded with your own thought life and your own opinions, and you're trying to find your way through this Christianity, but you haven't released yourself from the chains of what your mom or dad has said. See, some of you are having problems with how you were raised. Now, I'm not talking about all of you.

Most of us have had great family experiences, good memories, great Godly parents, and that kind of thing, but some of you have been abused. You have been lied to. You were rejected by a father or a mother; you've had severe issues in your childhood, and you didn't realize that momma could put a chain on you.

As I was preaching this sermon in my church, I had a story come to mind. I won't name the name, and the person knows who I'm talking about, but he won't mind me sharing his struggle and his victory with you. This man had a call on his life, and he went to his family to ask for their advice. The parents said, "Don't quit your day job." They put a chain on him that he had to break. He had to seek God's calling and purpose and not remain in that prison of hesitation and fear. He had to break free from the "just in case-isms" to be who God destined him to be.

There's a lot of kids who have a call of God on their life, and they want to go to school to pursue that calling. Please forgive me. I don't want to get into your family business here, but sometimes, you can crush a child's calling by putting on a chain of "just in case-isms." You tell them to pursue a secondary choice just in case the ministry doesn't work out. You encourage them to attend a different school just in case the money issues don't pan out. You put chains of fear, carnal reasoning and personal opinions on them that they were never meant to carry.

You see, the Bible says when the disciples followed Christ that they immediately left their nets, which means, "I'm going to go with you, and if it doesn't work out, I lose it all." Because sometimes, a chain can give you security, and a chain can give you a place of comfort. However, if you're to find freedom, you're going to have to come out from that cave of comfort. You're going to have to step beyond that graveyard of security to become who God has called you to be.

Some of you have held onto an opinion from someone who told you not to pursue God's best in your life, but to be free, you'll have to shake off those chains at all costs or it very well may cost you more than you were willing to pay.

When we lived in Monroe, we had some kids in our neighborhood who would come to swim and hang out with the boys. We had a little "swimming pool revival" on Kingridge in Monroe, Georgia. The boys would invite all their friends from the neighborhood to come to swim, and then they would invite them to church. Those neighborhood boys started going to church with my boys, and after a few months of their going to church, and the parents appreciating them going to that Pentecostal church, those little boys said, "We want to be baptized."

So, we scheduled them to be baptized, but then, grandma
got upset. The statements was made, "Well, if you're going to
get baptized, you don't need to get baptized in that church! I
mean, after all, your daddy was raised in this church. This is
where you should come if you're going to get baptized." Then,
one by one, all of the children backslid. That chain of religion
crushed their little faith.

Eventually, marriages busted up and families split apart.
One of the families moved out of the neighborhood and lost
everything they owned. Why? Because sometimes there's a
chain of what you should be based on how you were raised.

Please forgive me. I'm going to name names for a moment.
They say, "You can't act that way! You were raised Baptist.
You can't act that way! You're supposed to be Methodist. You
can't act that way! You're supposed to be Presbyterian. You're
supposed to be liturgical. You're Catholic; you're not supposed
to act that way." These statements are emphasized with even
more opinions, "When you get in that church and get around
all those people, all the graveyard people, people who came
running out of tombs, people who broke all those chains,
you'll see. You don't want to get around all those crazy people.
I've been there. They're sitting all clothed and in their right
mind, but I know who they used to be."

Listen to me, you can accept that bondage, and it will become codependency until you put all of your children in the same graveyard prison. I don't care what label you put on it. Put whatever denominational label on it that fits; there are some people who can't be Pentecostal because they're "Church of God." It doesn't matter the category, the denomination or the so-called heritage; it's all just a chain of religion and traditionalism.

There were two churches in a small town. One was a Baptist Church and one was a Christian Church. They were going to combine these churches. One of the elders of the Baptist church stood up and said, "I've been a Baptist my whole life. You're not about to make a Christian out of me!" That joke was told by Pastor Glen Money, at First Baptist Church, in Monroe, Georgia. Listen, if you keep living by what he says/ she says, and by what daddy did and what momma said, you're going to put everyone out there, screaming and crying in the graveyard. You're going to chain everyone with your religion and your rules of false expectations, opinions, and you will constantly beat people down.

I also need to say a word to some parents here. You're so committed to reliving your glory years that you refuse to let your kids be better than you are. You constantly tear them down because they haven't given you proper applause for the trophies that are in your trophy case. Nobody cares about your crusty, old trophies anymore. Listen, if you still needed all of that, you shouldn't have had children, but if you have babies, when they come in this world, it's not about whether you can fly like Superman. It's not about your fame and fortune anymore.

Quit putting chains on those babies and cut them loose. I need someone reading this to say, "I'm tired of stuff being put on me. I may not be right with God, but I'm not taking the junk they're putting on me. I know that I'm not where I should be, but I'm not accepting the rules or the regulations that they're trying to place on my life. I'm going to be who God called me to be."

He sat up all night cutting himself, crying. It occurred to me if you read the Scriptures, Jesus was up at night praying, too. Matter of fact, the miracles which preceded this one were preparatory miracles. If you study how this miracle occurred, you can see that Jesus was preparing himself.

Now, I'll bring you the information later once I have it completely studied out, but this man was used by Christ to initiate a revival. He was a wild man. When it was over with, this was the only time a person came to Jesus and said, "Can I be your disciple? I want to follow you." Jesus said, "No. You go home. Go home and tell them what's happened. Find your mom; find your dad and tell them your story."

You know what God told me to tell you today, mama? God's going to go get your baby out of that graveyard. He's going to send your child home. And when that baby comes home, they're going to be clothed and in their right mind. Listen to me, daddy. Those demons are coming out. What you've been frustrated with in the past, you just wait until God is finished casting the devil out of them. What Satan meant for evil, God meant for good. It's going to happen. I declare it, in the name of Jesus.

I'll tell you something more I really like about this story. The Bible says, "When he saw Jesus afar off." I guess, there's a good point to be made about people who can see Him coming. Some of you, you can't even tell He was beside you after He passes by.

Have you ever been in a worship service, and you're having a good time until you look at somebody else's face? You feel like responding, "Oh, dear Lord! Is your cellphone that interesting? Are your fingernails that beautiful?"

You're sitting there, thinking you're having a wonderful church service, and then you see them. Well, they couldn't tell if God were to come into the room and hit them with a 2x4. They can't tell that God's been in the house.

I like to get around people who just break stuff. I get those kinds of folks in my office before each worship service. Every one of the guys that pray for me before the service, they were in graveyards when God found them. The devil had to get cast out before you could even get them in church, and they bring the house down in prayer. They come ready to do serious business in prayer and in worship, and they help prepare me to bring forth the Word.

He saw Him from afar off. How many of you reading this can feel like you see Jesus when He's coming? See, that's what's happening in America right now. I don't know if you've been watching, but it's coming. There's a move of God. Something is going on in the heavenlies. I'm telling you, something's happening in downtown Jerusalem. There's a revival breaking out all over the world. You can feel the rumbling of rain coming. I can feel the power of God beginning to move on His people one more time. The foundations of His Church are being shaken.

They had a big, well-known speaker scheduled in Pigeon Forge for an upcoming student event in 2020, and he had to cancel. I don't remember what happened, but the spot was vacated. So, Kanye West and Lecrae joined up, and they're going to Pigeon Forge at the beginning of 2020.

Who knew? I saw this headline on Justin Bieber today. "I'm right where God wants me to be now. I'm singing songs to the glory of God." You might ask, "Pastor, do you think these things will hold up?" Honestly, I don't know. It might hold up as much as yours has.

Think about it. How many times do you flip and flop in and out of your faith? How many times have you failed? Don't be making fun of people in graveyards. You don't know what God can do. You don't know how many devils He can cast out with one word. He can take someone who is so lost and save their soul. He can take somebody who is demon-possessed and make them whole. I can see Him coming, and I see Him from afar off.

The Bible says he ran. Oh God, give us somebody who runs in. Give us someone who can't wait to get there, somebody who can say one more time, "I was glad when they said unto me, 'Let us go to the house of the Lord.'"

Give us someone, Heavenly Father, who sees you coming, and they can't wait to get into Your presence. Give us someone who doesn't hold back, someone who breaks the chains that try to weigh them down, someone who runs to you for deliverance.

This next part is the most encouraging of the Scripture to me, it says, "He fell down and worshipped Him." And Jesus didn't stop him. This man worshipped God while he was still crazy. That's some good praise. This man worshipped while he was still a drug addict. This man worshipped before he got saved. This man worshipped while he was still demon-possessed. Are you catching this? This man wasn't qualified. This man wasn't even connected to his family anymore. This man didn't look right, act right, talk right, live right, nothing; yet, he was still allowed to get in the presence of Jesus and worship.

This story lets me know there's a place for me at the feet of Jesus today. If that man, with cuts all over his arm, chains broken all over the graveyard, relationships busted from there all the way to the Gadarenes, if that man could praise God, then I say on this good, last Sunday of 2019, I believe I can praise God!

If he, in his busted condition, had enough eyesight to see Jesus, then surely, with all of my Bible reading and my Biblical understanding and my friendships and the anointing on my life, I can trust that where two or three are gathered together, He's right there in the middle of them. (Matthew 18:20)

So, I'll say this. If this chain-breaking grave bandit could glorify God, then the devil was a liar when he told me I'm not worthy. The devil says you're not worthy. The devil says you can't praise God and that you don't have your act together. The devil says you can't praise God; you weren't raised that way. The devil says you can't praise God because you've had too many chains in your life.

If this guy can run out of that graveyard, then I can lift my hands. If he can run out of that graveyard, then I can shout, "Hallelujah." If he can run out of that graveyard and call Jesus the Son of God, then I can say, "Jesus, the Son of God." Do I have any chain-breakers reading this today? Is there someone ready to run out of a graveyard right now? Let's run to the feet of Jesus!

About the Author

Joey Grizzle is the senior pastor at Buford Church of God in Buford, Ga. He and his wife, Mia, have been pastoring for 20 years and have been in the ministry for almost 27 years. He attended Lee University, where he met Mia and fell in love. They love chasing waterfalls, hiking mountainsides and seeking out new and exciting adventures all around the globe. They reside in Buford with their two sons.